A Shorter Course in

English Idiomatic Expressions

『5分間 英語イディオム表現』

Hidehiko Konaka

NAN'UN-DO

A Shorter Course in English Idiomatic Expressions

Copyright © 2015

Hidehiko Konaka

All rights Reserved

*No part of this book may be reproduced in any form without written permission
from the author and Nan'un-do Co., Ltd.*

はしがき

　イディオム表現とは，ある言語に特有の表現や固有の決まり文句です。英語はイディオム表現に富んだ言語といえます。例えば，bury the hatchet は「手斧を土に埋める」という意味ですが，和睦のしるしに武器である手斧を土の中に埋めたアメリカ先住民の風習に由来していて「和睦する」という意味で日常的に使われます。このようなイディオム表現を知らないと，英字新聞，ニュース雑誌，エッセイなどを読み進むこともできませんし，英米人の日常会話となると，なおさら理解できません。

　本テキストは，特に日常生活でよく使われるイディオム表現を収集し，それらを効率よく学べるように編集しました。本テキストは 20 のレッスンで構成されていますが，どのレッスンも同じ構成になっています。各セクションについて簡単に説明しておきます。

LET'S LEARN

日常生活でよく使われるイディオム表現です。例文の和訳を完成させる英文和訳問題になっています。すべての表現と例文を何度も音読して，きちんと自分のものにしましょう。

LET'S TRY

[A] 辞書定義に合うイディオム表現を選ぶ選択問題です。
[B] 下線部のイディオム表現の意味に最も近い語句を選ぶ選択問題です。
[C] 語句を並べかえ，英文を完成させる整序作文問題です。
[D] イディオム表現を含んだ英文を完成させ，和訳する英文和訳問題です。

　本テキストの編集にあたり，各種辞書類，参考書など多くの文献を参考にさせていただきました。本テキストはこれらの文献に負うところが多いことを記して謝辞といたします。

　本テキストが，英語をきちんと学び直したいという皆さんのお役に立てば，著者としてこれにすぎる喜びはありません。心から皆さんのご健闘をお祈りいたします。

　最後になりましたが，本テキストの編集・出版にあたり，いろいろお世話になった加藤敦氏に深く感謝いたします。また，Lynn Eve Harris 氏にすべての英文をていねいにチェックしていただき，適切なアドバイスもたくさんいただきました。心からお礼申し上げます。

2014 年 初夏
著者

Contents

LESSON 1	「天体・天候」を用いたイディオム表現	6
	「雲の中に頭を突っ込んでいる」ってどんな状態？	
LESSON 2	「空気・水」を用いたイディオム表現	8
	「空中を歩く」ってどんな気分？	
LESSON 3	「地・火」を用いたイディオム表現	10
	「世界に火をつける」って何をすること？	
LESSON 4	「自然」を用いたイディオム表現	12
	「丘を越えて」ってどんな状態？	
LESSON 5	「時」を用いたイディオム表現	14
	「それを1日と呼ぶ」って何をすること？	
LESSON 6	「植物」を用いたイディオム表現	16
	「丸太のコブのように」ってどんな状態？	
LESSON 7	「鳥」などを用いたイディオム表現	18
	「カラスが飛ぶように」ってどういう意味？	
LESSON 8	「動物」を用いたイディオム表現	20
	「ワニの涙を流す」って何をすること？	
LESSON 9	「色」を用いたイディオム表現 (1)	22
	「緑の親指をもっている」人ってどんな人？	
LESSON 10	「色」を用いたイディオム表現 (2)	24
	「赤い手のまま捕まえる」ってどういう意味？	

LESSON 11	「数字」を用いたイディオム表現		26
	「エイトボールの後ろにある」ってどんな状態？		
LESSON 12	「衣服」などを用いたイディオム表現		28
	「濡れた毛布を投げる」って何をすること？		
LESSON 13	「道具・武器」を用いたイディオム表現		30
	「丸い穴に四角いくぎ」の人ってどんな人？		
LESSON 14	「家具」などを用いたイディオム表現		32
	「戸棚の中の骸骨」って何？		
LESSON 15	「家屋」などを用いたイディオム表現		34
	「頭が天井にぶつかる」ってどうなること？		
LESSON 16	「食べ物」を用いたイディオム表現		36
	「ひとくちのケーキ」って何？		
LESSON 17	「飲食」を用いたイディオム表現 (1)		38
	「酸っぱいブドウ」って何？		
LESSON 18	「飲食」を用いたイディオム表現 (2)		40
	「リンゴを磨く」って何をすること？		
LESSON 19	「身体」を用いたイディオム表現 (1)		42
	「全部の指が親指」の人ってどんな人？		
LESSON 20	「身体」を用いたイディオム表現 (2)		44
	「耳の後ろが濡れている」ってどういうこと？		

LESSON 1 　「天体・天候」を用いたイディオム表現

「雲の中に頭を突っ込んでいる」ってどんな状態？

LET'S LEARN　下線部を埋め，和訳を完成させてみよう。

☐ ① **BE ON CLOUD NINE**　とても幸せである
  * アメリカ気象庁の雲の分類では，cloud nine は 3〜4 万フィート上空まで達する積乱雲で，その雲の上は「最高に嬉しい状態」を意味することから。

  ［例］Bob has been on cloud nine since he got promoted.
  　　（**1.** _____ ウキウキしているね）

☐ ② **HAVE ONE'S HEAD IN THE CLOUDS**　うわの空である；現実離れしている
  * 「雲の中に頭を突っ込んでいる」→「非現実的な世界に浸っている」

  ［例］Jane has her head in the clouds all day. She must be in love.
  　　（ジェーンは一日中うわの空だった。彼女は **2.** _____ ）

☐ ③ **HAVE STARS IN ONE'S EYES**　夢見心地になる
  * 夢を見ている状況を「星をじっと見ている」という言葉で表せることから。

  ［例］You've had stars in your eyes since you first saw him.
  　　（**3.** _____ 夢見心地になったんだね）

☐ ④ **ONCE IN A BLUE MOON**　きわめてまれに
  * アメリカの農業暦によると，約 2.5 年に 1 回 Blue Moon があるとされ，その「めったにない」Blue Moon に由来。

  ［例］You will only get a chance like this once in a blue moon.
  　　（こんなチャンスはめったにないよ）

☐ ⑤ **REACH FOR THE STARS**　実現不可能なことを企てる
  * 星に手を伸ばして取ることは不可能なことから。

☐ ⑥ **THANK ONE'S LUCKY STARS**　運が良くてありがたいと思う
  * 昔の人は，星が正しい配列になった時に幸運が訪れると考え，実際に幸運が訪れた時には，正しい配列になった星全体に感謝したことから。

  ［例］I thanked my lucky stars that I was a bachelor.
  　　（私は自分が独身であることを運命の星に感謝した）

☐ ⑦ **CALM BEFORE THE STORM**　嵐の前の静けさ
  * 「嵐の前の静けさ」→「騒動や危機が起こる前の平穏な時」

☐ ⑧ **UNDER THE WEATHER**　気分がすぐれない
  * 「天気に影響される」→「具合がよくない」

  ［例］How have you been?—I've been under the weather, but I'm better now.
  　　（「元気だった？」「このところ調子が悪くてね。でもだいぶよくなってきたよ」）

[A] 辞書定義に合うイディオム表現を選んでみよう。

1. be filled with happiness = _____

2. feel thankful for being fortunate = _____

3. plan to do something impossible to carry out = _____

[B] 下線部のイディオム表現の意味に合うものを選んでみよう。

1. Earthquakes occur in this area only <u>once in a blue moon</u>.
   (A) occasionally   (B) quite often   (C) very rarely

2. I'm a bit <u>under the weather</u> today, so I can't go to the office.
   (A) busy   (B) sick   (C) sleepy

3. You <u>have your head in the clouds</u>! It's time to face reality!
   (A) are absent-minded   (B) depend on me   (C) bother me

[C] 語句を並べかえ，英文を完成させてみよう。

1. 彼女は憧れのロックスターに声をかけられ，舞い上がっている。
   She [because / cloud / her / her favorite / nine / on / rock star / spoke / to / was].

   She _____.

2. 火事が発生したときに私が眠っていなかったことは，すごく幸運だったと思う。
   I [asleep when / broke / I / my lucky / out / stars that / thank / the fire / wasn't].

   I _____.

[D] 英文を完成させ，日本語に直してみよう。

1. The boss seemed strangely calm as I tried to explain my failure, but I felt that it was merely the calm before the (   ).

   _____

2. My sister has her head in the (   ) if she thinks she is going to become a cabin attendant. She is terrible at English.

   _____

7

LESSON 2　「空気・水」を用いたイディオム表現

「空中を歩く」ってどんな気分？

LET'S LEARN　下線部を埋め，和訳を完成させてみよう。

☐ ① **AS LIGHT AS AIR**　とても軽い；とても気楽な

＊「空気のように軽い」→「気分が晴れ晴れとして」

［例］My mobile phone is as light as air.
（僕の携帯電話は空気のように軽いんだ）

☐ ② **BE IN HOT WATER**　困っている

＊「熱湯の中にいる」→「窮地に陥っている」

＊ be in deep water とも表現できる。

［例］The boss found my accounting error. I'm in hot water.
（1.＿＿＿＿＿＿＿＿＿＿＿＿＿＿＿＿＿＿＿＿。厄介なことになったわ）

☐ ③ **GO THROUGH FIRE AND WATER**　あらゆる危険を覚悟する

＊ 危険を象徴する2大要素の「火」と「水」の中を通って行くことから。

☐ ④ **HOLD WATER**　つじつまが合う；筋が通る

＊「容器が水を一滴も漏らさない」→「筋道が通っている」

［例］I don't think the police's theory will hold water. The suspect has an alibi.
（警察の説明は筋が通っていないと思うよ。2.＿＿＿＿＿＿＿＿＿＿＿＿＿＿＿＿＿＿）

☐ ⑤ **KEEP ONE'S HEAD ABOVE WATER**　財政的に何とかやっていく

＊「溺れないように顔を水面から出している」→「借金せずに何とかやっていく」

［例］Our office managed to keep its head above water by securing a bank loan.
（わが社は銀行からの融資を取りつけることでどうにかやっていくことができた）

☐ ⑥ **MAKE ONE'S MOUTH WATER**　食欲をそそる；欲しがらせる

＊「よだれを流させる」→「気をそそる」

［例］The mere mention of pizza made my mouth water.
（3.＿＿＿＿＿＿＿＿＿＿＿＿＿＿＿＿＿＿よだれが出てきた）

☐ ⑦ **PUT ON AIRS**　気取る；もったいぶる

＊ この airs は「気取った態度」「もったいぶる振る舞い」という意味。

［例］He puts on airs about his education.
（彼は学歴をひどく鼻にかけている）

☐ ⑧ **WALK ON AIR**　ウキウキする

＊「空中を歩く」→「高揚している」

［例］Since we've decided to spend Christmas in Rome, they've been walking on air.
（クリスマスをローマで過ごすことに決めてから，彼らは有頂天になっている）

8

[A]　辞書定義に合うイディオム表現を選んでみよう。

1. act superior = _____

2. be able to be proved = _____

3. be prepared for all sorts of dangers = _____

[B]　下線部のイディオム表現の意味に合うものを選んでみよう。

1. Anne was <u>walking on air</u> when she got the job.
   (A) furious　　　　(B) so exhausted　　　　(C) very happy

2. I'm not rich, but I've managed to <u>keep my head above water</u>.
   (A) be well paid　　(B) get by　　　　　　(C) live alone

3. When we heard that all of the victims were rescued, we felt <u>as light as air</u>.
   (A) lonely　　　　 (B) relieved　　　　　 (C) sorrow

[C]　語句を並べかえ，英文を完成させてみよう。

1. タンポポは種がとても軽いので，かなり遠くまで広がっていく。
   Dandelions [air / are / as / as / because / light / so far / spread / their / seeds].

   Dandelions _____.

2. 昔のカノジョに会ったことで，彼は妻との関係が厄介なことになった。
   Meeting [girlfriend / him / his wife / hot water / landed / an old / in / with].

   Meeting _____.

[D]　英文を完成させ，日本語に直してみよう。

1. She is always putting on (　　　　　　　) and pretending she comes from a good family.

   _____

2. Just looking at the pictures in the cookbook is enough to make my mouth (　　　　　　).

   _____

LESSON 3 「地・火」を用いたイディオム表現

「世界に火をつける」って何をすること？

LET'S LEARN　下線部を埋め，和訳を完成させてみよう。

① **ADD FUEL TO THE FIRE**　火に油を注ぐ
* 「火に燃料を加える」→「問題を悪化させる」
* add fuel to the flame とも表現できる。

[例] Brad tried to calm her down by telling a joke, but it only added fuel to the fire.
（ブラッドは冗談を言って彼女をなだめようとしたが，かえって火に油を注いだ）

② **BUILD A FIRE UNDER ～**　～をその気にさせる
* 相手を自分の思い通りに行動させるために，相手のお尻の下に薪をくべて火をたくイメージから。

[例] Mother built a fire under me and got me to go on an errand.
（母はせき立てて私をお使いに行かせた）

③ **COME DOWN TO EARTH**　現実に戻る；現実的になる
* 鳥のように大空を羽ばたいている状態から地上に降りて，現実の世界に戻るイメージから。

[例] It was difficult to come back down to earth after our marvelous vacation in Tahiti.
（タヒチですばらしい休暇を過ごした後で，日常の生活に戻るのは難しかった）

④ **DOWN-TO-EARTH**　現実的な；社会常識があって
* 「大地に根を下ろして」→「地に足がついて」

[例] The committee's plans for the town are anything but down-to-earth.
（1. _____ は少しも現実的ではない）

⑤ **GAIN GROUND**　人気を得る
* 「敵地を獲得する」→「進出して広げる」

[例] Our new product is gaining ground against that of our competitor.
（2. _____ 人気を得ている）

⑥ **MOVE HEAVEN AND EARTH**　大変な努力をする
* 「天地を動かす」→「どんなことでもする」

[例] I'll move heaven and earth to make you happy.
（3. _____ だったら何でもするよ）

⑦ **SET THE WORLD ON FIRE**　世間をあっと言わせる
* 「世界に火をつける」→「目覚ましい業績を上げて世間をあっと言わせる」

⑧ **TO THE ENDS OF THE EARTH**　地の果てまで
* 「地球の端まで」→「地の果てまで」

LET'S TRY

[A]　辞書定義に合うイディオム表現を選んでみよう。

◯ 1. become more important or popular = _____

◯ 2. say or do something that makes a bad situation worse

= _____

◯ 3. to the remotest and most inaccessible points on the earth

= _____

[B]　下線部のイディオム表現の意味に合うものを選んでみよう。

◯ 1. Your new plan is wonderful, but you must come down to earth.
　　(A) be ambitious　　(B) be realistic　　(C) be responsible

◯ 2. Fred had to move heaven and earth to finish the job on schedule.
　　(A) ask for help　　(B) skip lunch　　(C) work hard

◯ 3. I admire him for his down-to-earth approach to problem-solving.
　　(A) novel　　(B) practical　　(C) up-to-date

[C]　語句を並べかえ，英文を完成させてみよう。

◯ 1. 泣いている子に大声をあげるのは火に油を注ぐようなものだ。
　　Shouting [a / at / child / crying / fuel / just adds / the fire / to].

　　Shouting _____.

◯ 2. 彼は勤勉な人だが，どう見ても将来有名になるようなことはやりそうもない。
　　I [but he / fire / guess he / is / hard-working, / will never / on / set / the world].

　　I _____.

[D]　英文を完成させ，日本語に直してみよう。

◯ 1. I love him very much. If he asked me, I'd follow him to the ends of the
　　(　　　　　　).

_____

◯ 2. Our daughter doesn't study as much as she should. I wish we could build
　　a (　　　　　　) under her.

LESSON 4 「自然」を用いたイディオム表現

「丘を越えて」ってどんな状態？

LET'S LEARN　下線部を埋め，和訳を完成させてみよう。

□ ① **BE AT SEA**　困っている

＊海上では嵐にあったり，座礁したりと困ることが多いことから。

＊「航海中で」という意味もある。

［例］I was all at sea about how to carry out the sales campaign for our new product.
（自社の 1._____ 全くわからない）

□ ② **BE ON THE ROCKS**　破たんしている；破産している

＊「船が座礁している」→「進退きわまっている」

［例］Their marriage is on the rocks.
（彼らの結婚生活は破たんしている）

□ ③ **BE OUT LIKE A LIGHT**　突然意識を失って

＊「光のようにパッと消えて」→「突然意識不明になって」

＊ be out cold とも表現できる。

［例］She fell down on the icy road, hit her head, and she was out like a light.
（2._____ 頭を打ち，あっという間に気を失った）

□ ④ **BE OVER THE HILL**　盛りを過ぎている

＊「丘を越えて」→「人生の盛んな時を過ぎて」

□ ⑤ **BREAK THE ICE**　緊張や堅苦しさをほぐす；突破口を作る

＊砕氷船（ice breaker）が氷を砕いて，他の船が楽に通れるようにすることから。

［例］The atmosphere of the meeting was quite stiff, but Ed broke the ice with a joke.
（3._____，エドのジョークで緊張が解けた）

□ ⑥ **OUT OF THE WOODS**　危険を切り抜けて

＊森は暗く，神秘的で，時には道に迷いやすく危険な場所とみなされていることから。

［例］When a patient reaches this stage, he is out of the woods.
（患者がこの段階に達すると危機を脱したことになる）

□ ⑦ **SELL ～ DOWN THE RIVER**　～を裏切る

＊昔，ミシシッピー川上流の農園主が，必要なくなった奴隷を裏切って下流の農園に売り払ったことに由来。

［例］He sold me down the river so he could be general manager.
（彼は自分が部長になるために，僕を裏切ったんだ）

□ ⑧ **THE TIP OF THE ICEBERG**　氷山の一角

＊氷の先端部分は浮かんでいる氷山全体のほんの一部にすぎないことから。

12

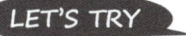

[A] 辞書定義に合うイディオム表現を選んでみよう。

☐ 1. go bankrupt = _____

☐ 2. past a critical phase = _____

☐ 3. initiate social interchanges and conversation = _____

[B] 下線部のイディオム表現の意味に合うものを選んでみよう。

☐ 1. My best friend sold me down the river the other day.
　　(A) apologized to me　　(B) betrayed me　　(C) scolded me

☐ 2. After he was given a strong anesthetic, the patient was out like a light.
　　(A) became energetic　　(B) fell unconscious　　(C) felt depressed

☐ 3. When it comes to even the simplest cooking, Kevin is hopelessly at sea.
　　(A) confused　　(B) outstanding　　(C) persistent

[C] 語句を並べかえ，英文を完成させてみよう。

☐ 1. その2国の関係は暗礁に乗り上げているようだ。
Relations [appear / be / between / countries / on / the rocks / the two / to].

Relations _____.

☐ 2. ジムはマラソンを完走し，まだまだやれることを証明した。
Jim [and / finished / he / proved / over / the hill / the marathon / wasn't / yet].

Jim _____.

[D] 英文を完成させ，日本語に直してみよう。

☐ 1. This large expenditure is only the tip of the (_____) with regard to total party spending on the election.

_____

☐ 2. Ever since Henry Ford broke the (_____) in the manufacture of automobiles, mass production has been indispensable to the industrial world.

_____

13

LESSON 5　「時」を用いたイディオム表現

「それを1日と呼ぶ」って何をすること？

LET'S LEARN　下線部を埋め，和訳を完成させてみよう。

☐ ① **AS SURELY AS NIGHT FOLLOWS DAY**　必ず

＊ 昼の後に必ず夜が来ることから。

［例］Success follows diligence as surely as night follows day.
（勤勉のあとには必ず成功が訪れる）

☐ ② **BURN THE MIDNIGHT OIL**　夜遅くまで勉強する

＊ 電気が発明される前，深夜まで勉強するためにランプに油で火をともしたことから。

［例］If you burn the midnight oil night after night, you'll probably become ill.
（毎晩夜更かしして頑張っていると 1._____ ）

☐ ③ **CALL IT A DAY**　仕事を切り上げる

＊「それを1日と呼ぶ」→「それで1日分は終わったとする」

［例］I'm tired. Let's call it a day.
（私は疲れた。今日はこのへんで切り上げよう）

☐ ④ **COUNT THE DAYS**　心待ちにする

＊「日を数える」→「指折り数えて待つ」

［例］We used to count the days until Christmas when we were children.
（子どもの頃は，クリスマスがくるのを指折り数えて待ったものです）

☐ ⑤ **HAVE SPRING FEVER**　春先の落ち着かない気分になる

＊「春の熱」→「寒い冬が終わり，何か楽しいことをしたいという落ち着かない気分」

☐ ⑥ **PLAY FOR TIME**　時間稼ぎをする

＊「時間を得るために何かをする」→「理由をつけて時間稼ぎをする」

［例］Don't try to play for time by telling me lies.
（2._____ 時間稼ぎをしようとしてもダメだよ）

☐ ⑦ **SAVE ～ FOR A RAINY DAY**　まさかの時のために～を蓄える

＊「雨の日のために蓄える」→「将来のために取っておく」

［例］Don't spend all of your money. You should save something for a rainy day.
（3._____ 。まさかの時に備えて少しは蓄えておくのよ）

☐ ⑧ **THE MORNING AFTER**　二日酔い

＊ the morning after の後ろに the night before が省略されていて，「前の晩の活動からくる悪い結果」で，特に「二日酔い」を意味する。

［例］A headache is often a symptom of the morning after.
（頭痛は二日酔いのよくある徴候の1つだ）

14

LET'S TRY

[A]　辞書定義に合うイディオム表現を選んでみよう。

◯ 1. quit work and go home = _____

◯ 2. stay up studying late at night = _____

◯ 3. have a lazy feeling when the weather starts to become warmer
 = _____

[B]　下線部のイディオム表現の意味に合うものを選んでみよう。

◯ 1. We used to count the days until New Year's Day when we were children.
　　(A) look forward to　　(B) put up with　　(C) stand up for

◯ 2. Economic recession follows economic prosperity as surely as night follows day.
　　(A) in short order　　(B) then and there　　(C) without fail

◯ 3. I got too drunk last night, my upset stomach is a result of the morning after.
　　(A) a bad cold　　(B) a hangover　　(C) a stomachache

[C]　語句を並べかえ，英文を完成させてみよう。

◯ 1. 4月に雪が解けると，また春先の落ち着かない気分になります。
　　After [again / April, / fever once / have / melts in / spring / the snow / we'll].

　　After _____ .

◯ 2. ゆうべ遅くまでかかって所得税の申告書を作った。
　　I [burnt / last / my income / night filling out / oil / tax forms / the midnight].

　　I _____ .

[D]　英文を完成させ，日本語に直してみよう。

◯ 1. We never spend my husband's bonus. We always save it for a rainy
　　(　　　　　).

　　_____

◯ 2. There was no reason why they couldn't have signed the contract right away. They were
　　only playing for (　　　　　) in hopes of making a better deal elsewhere.

15

LESSON 6 「植物」を用いたイディオム表現

「丸太のコブのように」ってどんな状態？

LET'S LEARN　下線部を埋め，和訳を完成させてみよう。

☐ ① **BARK UP THE WRONG TREE**　見当違いのことをする
   * アライグマ狩りで，猟犬がアライグマを木の上に追い詰めて，その獲物が隣の木に移ってしまったのに，その獲物がいなくなった木を見上げて吠えることから。
   ［例］If you think it was me who revealed the secret, you're barking up the wrong tree.
   （1._____と考えているならお門違いだ）

☐ ② **BE UP A TREE**　非常に困っている
   * 獣が逃げるために，木に登った結果，逃げ場を失うことから。

☐ ③ **BEAT AROUND THE BUSH**　遠回しに言う
   * 「茂みの周りを叩いて獲物の鳥を追い出す」→「さぐりを入れる」
   * beat about the bush とも表現できる。
   ［例］Tell me the truth; don't beat around the bush.
   （遠回しに言わないで，2._____）

☐ ④ **LIKE A BUMP ON A LOG**　ボーッとして
   * 「材木として役に立たない丸太のコブのように」→「役に立たずにボーッとして」
   ［例］Don't sit there like a bump on a log. Give me a hand.
   （ボーッとそこに座っていないで，手伝ってよ）

☐ ⑤ **NIP 〜 IN THE BUD**　〜を早い段階で終わらせる
   * 「つぼみのうちに摘み取る」→「初期の段階で断ち切ってしまう」
   ［例］Early detection of disease allows doctors to nip it in the bud.
   （3._____，医者は病気を早い段階で断ち切ることができる）

☐ ⑥ **NO BED OF ROSES**　楽なものではないこと
   * 「バラを敷き詰めたベッドではないこと」→「安楽な境遇ではないこと」
   ［例］This job is no bed of roses. There are lots of things I don't like about it.
   （この仕事だって楽じゃない。気に入らないことがたくさんあるから）

☐ ⑦ **ROOT AND BRANCH**　徹底的に
   * 「木の重要な部分としての根，発展した部分としての枝も何もかも」→「完全に」
   ［例］The police put an end to the smuggling, root and branch.
   （警察はその密輸を根絶した）

☐ ⑧ **TURN OVER A NEW LEAF**　心を入れ替える
   * 「本の新しいページをめくる」→「フレッシュなスタートを切る」

[A] 辞書定義に合うイディオム表現を選んでみよう。

☐ 1. no easy task = _____

☐ 2. make a wrong guess = _____

☐ 3. being useless by doing nothing = _____

[B] 下線部のイディオム表現の意味に合うものを選んでみよう。

☐ 1. It's time for you to <u>turn over a new leaf</u> and start exercising.
　　(A) make a change　　(B) make your way　　(C) take your time

☐ 2. To eliminate corruption <u>root and branch</u>, we need to make new laws.
　　(A) completely　　(B) gradually　　(C) officially

☐ 3. I'm <u>up a tree</u>, because I lost my driver's license and I have to drive to St. Louis.
　　(A) in haste　　(B) in trouble　　(C) in vain

[C] 語句を並べかえ，英文を完成させてみよう。

☐ 1. 心を入れ替えて，一生懸命勉強することにしたよ。
　　I've [a / decided / harder / and / new leaf / over / study / to / turn].

　　I've _____ .

☐ 2. 遠回しなものの言い方はやめて，仕事にとりかかろうじゃないか。
　　Let's [around / beating / get down to / business / stop / the bush and].

　　Let's _____ .

[D] 英文を完成させ，日本語に直してみよう。

☐ 1. The players blamed their bad records on the pitchers, but they were barking up the wrong (　　　　　　).

　　_____

☐ 2. Through a tip from an informant, the police were able to nip the planned bank robbery in the (　　　　　　).

　　_____

17

LESSON 7 「鳥」などを用いたイディオム表現

「カラスが飛ぶように」ってどういう意味？

LET'S LEARN　下線部を埋め，和訳を完成させてみよう。

☐ ① **AN EARLY BIRD**　早起きの人；早くに到着する人；素早く何かを始める人
  * The early bird catches the worm.（早起きの鳥は虫を捕まえる）に由来。
  〔例〕George is an early bird. He does his best work before 8 a.m.
  （ジョージは早起きだ。午前 8 時までに最もよく仕事をする）

☐ ② **AS THE CROW FLIES**　直線距離で
  * カラスは目標物に向かって一直線に飛ぶことから。
  〔例〕Our house is only a few miles from the lake as the crow flies.
  （わが家は直線距離で 1.＿＿＿＿＿＿＿＿＿＿＿＿＿＿＿＿＿＿＿＿）

☐ ③ **CHICKEN FEED**　はした金
  * ニワトリには売り物にならない穀物をエサとして与えたことから。
  〔例〕She's so rich that $1,000 is chicken feed to her.
  （2.＿＿＿＿＿＿＿＿＿＿＿＿＿＿＿＿＿，1,000 ドルなんてはした金さ）

☐ ④ **EAT LIKE A BIRD**　少食である
  * 小鳥はついばむ程度にしか食べないことから。
  * 逆の意味の表現に eat like a pig，eat like a horse がある。
  〔例〕Alice ate like a bird and spoke very little.
  （アリスは少食で口数も少なかった）

☐ ⑤ **HAVE A BEE IN ONE'S BONNET**　妙な固定観念をもっている
  * ある突拍子もない考えが浮かび，その考えが頭からなかなか離れないと，ハチが帽子の中で飛び回っているような感じがすることから。

☐ ⑥ **HAVE BUTTERFLIES IN ONE'S STOMACH**　ドキドキしている
  * ドキドキすると胃の中でチョウが舞っているような感じがすることから。
  〔例〕I have butterflies in my stomach before every speech.
  （3.＿＿＿＿＿＿＿＿＿＿＿＿＿＿＿＿いつもひどくあがってしまう）

☐ ⑦ **QUIT 〜 COLD TURKEY**　〜をスパッとやめる
  * 麻薬中毒者が麻薬をやめると，禁断症状のために鳥肌が立つことから。

☐ ⑧ **THE BIRDS AND THE BEES**　性の基礎知識
  * 子どもに性の話をするとき，ストレートに表現しづらいために，「鳥」や「ハチ」の交尾をたとえに出すことから。
  〔例〕My father tried to teach me about the birds and the bees.
  （父は私に性の基礎知識を教えようとした）

[A] 辞書定義に合うイディオム表現を選んでみよう。

☐ 1. in a straight line = _____

☐ 2. have an obsession = _____

☐ 3. someone who gets up or arrives early = _____

[B] 下線部のイディオム表現の意味に合うものを選んでみよう。

☐ 1. Cathy is trying to lose weight by eating <u>like a bird</u>.
　　(A) nothing　　　(B) too much　　　(C) very little

☐ 2. The salary at my first job was mere <u>chicken feed</u>.
　　(A) a fortune　　(B) a small amount of money　(C) easy money

☐ 3. I'm ready for today's speech, but I <u>have butterflies in my stomach</u>.
　　(A) am confident　(B) can hardly wait　　(C) feel uneasy

[C] 語句を並べかえ，英文を完成させてみよう。

☐ 1. 私はタバコをやめるのはほとんど不可能だとわかった。
I [almost / found / impossible / it / quit / smoking / to / cold turkey].

I _____ .

☐ 2. 上司に昇給を頼んだとき，緊張でドキドキした。
I [a raise / asked / butterflies / for / had / I / in / my stomach / when / the boss].

I _____ .

[D] 英文を完成させ，日本語に直してみよう。

☐ 1. Meg didn't know anything about the birds and the (　　　　　)
until she got married.

_____

☐ 2. Our house is only five miles from here as the (　　　　　) flies, but
the winding roads mean we have to drive nearly eight miles to get there.

_____

LESSON 8 「動物」を用いたイディオム表現

「ワニの涙を流す」って何をすること？

LET'S LEARN　下線部を埋め，和訳を完成させてみよう。

☐ ① **A DOG-EAT-DOG WORLD**　食うか食われるかの世界
  * ひどくお腹をすかしている獰猛な犬たちは，同じ食べ物を求めて熾烈な戦いを繰り広げることから。

☐ ② **BEAT A DEAD HORSE**　無駄な努力をする
  * どんなに強く叩いても死んだ馬は動かないことから。

☐ ③ **DRIVE ～ APE**　～を興奮させる
  *「～をサルにする」という意味。サルは好物のバナナを見せると興奮して騒ぎ回ることから。

☐ ④ **HAVE ANTS IN ONE'S PANTS**　何かしたくてウズウズしている
  *「ズボンの中にアリがいる」→「落ち着きがない」
  [例] Why do you have ants in your pants?—I'm going to meet my fiancé's parents for the first time.
  （「何でソワソワしているの？」「1.＿＿＿＿＿＿＿＿＿＿＿＿＿＿＿＿＿＿＿＿」）

☐ ⑤ **LET THE CAT OUT OF THE BAG**　うっかり秘密を漏らす
  * 昔，農村の市場では子豚を袋に入れて売る習慣があり，悪徳商人が子豚の代わりにネコを入れて売ろうとしたが，ネコが袋から出てばれてしまったことに由来。
  [例] It's a secret. Don't let the cat out of the bag.
  （それは秘密です。うっかり秘密を漏らさないようにしてね）

☐ ⑥ **LOOK A GIFT HORSE IN THE MOUTH**　もらい物のあらさがしをする
  * 馬は歯を見れば，その年齢や健康状態がわかることから。
  [例] I wasn't happy with my present, but I never look a gift horse in the mouth.
  （2.＿＿＿＿＿＿＿＿＿＿＿＿＿＿＿＿＿，もらい物にけちをつけられないね）

☐ ⑦ **SHED CROCODILE TEARS**　そら涙を流す
  * ワニは獲物を食べる時に，涙を流すと言われていることから。
  [例] She shed crocodile tears over his death.
  （彼女は彼の死にそら涙を流した）

☐ ⑧ **THE BLACK SHEEP OF THE FAMILY**　（一家・グループの）厄介者
  * 黒い羊は数が少ないため売れるほど毛を刈れず，ほかの色にも染まらないため羊飼いから嫌われていたことから。
  [例] He is the black sheep of the family. He's often in trouble with the police.
  （彼は一家のもてあまし者だ。3.＿＿＿＿＿＿＿＿＿＿＿＿＿＿＿＿＿＿＿）

[A] 辞書定義に合うイディオム表現を選んでみよう。

☐ 1. pretend that you are weeping = _____

☐ 2. find fault in something that is given to you = _____

☐ 3. waste time and effort trying to do something that cannot be done
  = _____

[B] 下線部のイディオム表現の意味に合うものを選んでみよう。

☐ 1. The thought of going out with Kay is driving me ape.
  (A) goes nowhere (B) makes me excited (C) keeps me cool

☐ 2. You have ants in your pants. Is something the matter?
  (A) are restless (B) get refreshed (C) look pale

☐ 3. We're going to throw a surprise party for Roger, but Alex let the cat out of the bag.
  (A) concealed it (B) ignored it (C) revealed it

[C] 語句を並べかえ，英文を完成させてみよう。

☐ 1. 彼に勘定を払わせようとするなんて無駄な努力だよ。
  You're [a / beating / dead horse / get / him / trying / pay / the bill / to / to].
  You're _____.

☐ 2. 最初に仕事をするようになったとき，なんて厳しい世界なんだろうと思った。
  When [dog-eat-dog / got / I / I / job, / my first / realized / what a / world it was].
  When _____.

[D] 英文を完成させ，日本語に直してみよう。

☐ 1. Mary sheds (_____) tears to get her way. You'd better watch out.
  _____

☐ 2. I hear he's the black (_____) of the family. He ran away at 16 to become an actor, and his parents never forgave him.
  _____

21

LESSON 9 「色」を用いたイディオム表現 (1)

「緑の親指をもっている」人ってどんな人？

LET'S LEARN　下線部を埋め，和訳を完成させてみよう。

☐ ① **BE GREEN WITH ENVY**　うらやましがっている；嫉妬している
* 嫉妬すると胆汁の分泌量が増えて，顔色が青ざめると考えられていたことに由来。
* be green with jealousy とも表現できる。

［例］He is green with envy because you have succeeded.
（1._____ 彼はひどくねたんでいる）

☐ ② **BORN IN THE PURPLE**　高貴の生れである
* 昔，王侯貴族が身にまとったとされる紫の衣を the purple ということから。

［例］It must be nice to be born in the purple like him.
（彼のように高貴な生まれだったらよかったのになあ）

☐ ③ **BROWN-NOSE**　へつらう；ごまをする
* 相手のお尻にキスをして，ウンチで茶色になるまでおべっかを使うイメージから。

☐ ④ **HAVE A GREEN THUMB**　植物を育てるのが上手である
* 植物を大切に育てていれば，自然とその指に植物の色が移っていくイメージから。

［例］He must have a green thumb. His garden is always beautiful.
（彼には園芸の才があるわ。2._____）

☐ ⑤ **IN BLACK AND WHITE**　文書にして；文字にして
*「黒（インク）と白（紙）で」→「言葉だけでなくきちんと文書にして」

［例］You shouldn't pay any money until you see the contract in black and white.
（契約をきちんと文書にするまではお金を払ってはいけない）

☐ ⑥ **IN THE RED [BLACK]**　赤字［黒字］になって
* 以前は，元帳の借方はすべて赤インクで，貸方は黒インクで記入していたことから。

［例］Our company is struggling to get back in the black.
（わが社は黒字に戻そうと苦闘している）

☐ ⑦ **OUT OF THE BLUE**　突然に
*「それまで青空以外のものは何も見えないところから」→「突然に」
* a bolt out of the blue（青天の霹靂）に由来。
* out of a clear sky とも表現できる。

［例］Out of the blue, I suddenly remembered his name.
（私は突然 3._____）

☐ ⑧ **WHITER THAN WHITE**　清廉潔白な
* 白のイメージは「罪がないこと」で，誠実さを象徴することから。

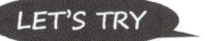

[A] 辞書定義に合うイディオム表現を選んでみよう。

1. born into a noble family = _____

2. printed, as in a contract = _____

3. absolutely honest and never do anything bad = _____

[B] 下線部のイディオム表現の意味に合うものを選んでみよう。

1. The messenger appeared in my office <u>out of the blue</u>.
   (A) intentionally　　(B) suddenly　　(C) unofficially

2. They say that our municipal finances are in <u>the red</u>.
   (A) a deficit　　(B) a surplus　　(C) high interest

3. I'm sick and tired of watching Rod <u>brown-nose</u> the teacher.
   (A) flatter　　(B) reject　　(C) stare at

[C] 語句を並べかえ、英文を完成させてみよう。

1. 彼女はおべっかを使えば昇進できると思っている。
   She [brown-nosing / by / can / get / promoted / seems / she / think / to].

   She _____.

2. 彼のそばにほかの女の子がいるとなぜか嫉妬しちゃうわ。
   Whenever [another girl / with envy / I'm green / is near him, / some reason / for].

   Whenever _____.

[D] 英文を完成させ、日本語に直してみよう。

1. My grandfather doesn't have a (　　　　　) thumb, which is why his houseplants are all dead.

   _____

2. I agree that their offer is too good to be true. I won't believe it until they put it down in (　　　　　) and white.

LESSON 10 「色」を用いたイディオム表現 (2)

「赤い手のまま捕まえる」ってどういう意味？

LET'S LEARN　下線部を埋め，和訳を完成させてみよう。

☐ ① **A WHITE ELEPHANT**　無用の長物
   * 白象はタイで神聖視され，飼うのに非常にお金がかかったため，王が臣下を失脚させるためにわざと白象を与えたことに由来。
   [例] The old computer my uncle gave me turned out to be a white elephant.
   （1.＿＿＿＿＿＿＿＿＿＿＿＿＿＿＿＿は無用の長物だったよ）

☐ ② **BE IN THE PINK**　元気でぴんぴんしている
   * ピンク色は赤ちゃんの肌の色を連想させ「若さ」や「健康」をイメージさせることから。

☐ ③ **BE NOT SO BLACK AS 〜 IS PAINTED**　〜は噂されているほど悪くない
   * 黒には「悪魔」のイメージがあり，悪いことを連想させることから。

☐ ④ **BE TICKLED PINK**　とても喜んでいる
   *「顔がピンク色になるまでくすぐられる」→「とても嬉しい」
   [例] I was tickled pink when your present arrived.
   （2.＿＿＿＿＿＿＿＿＿＿＿＿＿＿＿＿すごく嬉しかった）

☐ ⑤ **CATCH 〜 RED-HANDED**　〜を現行犯で逮捕する
   * 犯行現場から「血に染まった手」を連想させることから。
   [例] The police caught the criminal red-handed.
   （警察は犯人を現行犯で捕まえた）

☐ ⑥ **GIVE 〜 THE RED CARPET TREATMENT**　〜に最上のもてなしをする
   * 王族などの要人の公式訪問では，空港や公の建物に細長い赤いカーペットを敷いて迎えることから。

☐ ⑦ **SEE RED**　激怒する；かっとなる
   * 闘牛で，雄牛が赤い布きれやマントを見ると興奮して怒り狂うことから。
   [例] Well, I admit I saw red, and didn't much know what I was doing.
   （とにかく僕も認めるが，かっとなって自分が何をしているかよくわからなかったんだ）

☐ ⑧ **SHOW ONE'S TRUE COLORS**　本性を見せる
   * この colors は「国旗」を意味し，偽りの国旗のもと航行している船が「その国籍を明らかにする」がもともとの意味。
   [例] I don't know what Lucy is thinking. She never shows her true colors.
   （3.＿＿＿＿＿＿＿＿＿＿＿＿＿＿＿＿。彼女は本性を見せないから）

[A] 辞書定義に合うイディオム表現を選んでみよう。

◯ 1. be in high spirits = _____

◯ 2. be not so bad as ~ is rumored = _____

◯ 3. something that is useless and is either a nuisance or expensive to keep up
= _____

[B] 下線部のイディオム表現の意味に合うものを選んでみよう。

◯ 1. When I was late for the second time, my teacher saw red.
　　(A) felt nervous　　(B) was disappointed　　(C) was very angry

◯ 2. Susan was tickled pink that someone had remembered her birthday.
　　(A) astonished　　(B) filled with sorrow　　(C) very pleased

◯ 3. He was caught red-handed stealing, thanks to the informer's report to the police.
　　(A) arrested in the act of　(B) released from　　(C) sued for

[C] 語句を並べかえ，英文を完成させてみよう。

◯ 1. 私たちは計画が受け入れられたと聞いてすごく喜んでいます。
We [accepted / are / been / has / hear that / our plan / to / tickled pink].

We _____.

◯ 2. トムは，人気がある日本で盛大に歓迎された。
Tom [carpet treatment / given / he is / in Japan, where / popular / the red / was].

Tom _____.

[D] 英文を完成させ，日本語に直してみよう。

◯ 1. It's hard to tell what Julie is thinking. She never shows her true (　　　　　).

_____

◯ 2. The antique vase Aunt Mary gave me is a (　　　　　) elephant. It's huge and ugly.

_____

25

LESSON 11　「数字」を用いたイディオム表現

「エイトボールの後ろにある」ってどんな状態？

LET'S LEARN　下線部を埋め，和訳を完成させてみよう。

☐ ① **AT THE ELEVENTH HOUR**　土壇場で
　　＊ マタイによる福音書に出てくる，1日の11番目の時間（午後5時）に仕事を与えられた人の話に由来。

☐ ② **BE BEHIND THE EIGHT BALL**　不利な状態にいる
　　＊ あるビリヤードゲームでは，白玉が，当てると負けになるエイトボール（8の字が書かれた黒玉）の後ろにあると，ほかの玉を狙うのが難しくなることから。
　　〔例〕Michael is behind the eight ball. He can't quit his job because of his debts, but his new boss hates him and wants to fire him.
　　（マイケルは困っている。**1.**＿＿＿＿＿＿＿＿＿＿＿＿＿＿＿＿＿＿＿，新しい上司が彼を嫌っていて彼を首にしたがっているんだ）

☐ ③ **BE IN SEVENTH HEAVEN**　有頂天になっている
　　＊ seventh heaven（第7天国）は，ユダヤ人が考えた神と天使たちが住む最上天のことで「最も嬉しい状態」を表すことから。
　　〔例〕Ed was in seventh heaven; he had been given a bike for his birthday.
　　（エドはうれしくて有頂天だった。**2.**＿＿＿＿＿＿＿＿＿＿＿＿＿＿＿＿＿＿＿）

☐ ④ **DEEP-SIX ～**　～を処分する
　　＊ 土を6フィート（約1.8メートル）掘って死者を葬ったり，海で6尋（約11メートル）の深さに死者を水葬したことに由来。

☐ ⑤ **KILL TWO BIRDS WITH ONE STONE**　一石二鳥である
　　＊ 狩りの時，1つの石で2羽の鳥を打ち落とすことから。

☐ ⑥ **ON ALL FOURS**　四つんばいになって
　　＊「4つすべてを支点として」→「手と膝を使ってかがんで」
　　〔例〕Louis was looking for his earring on all fours.
　　（ルイスは四つんばいになって，**3.**＿＿＿＿＿＿＿＿＿＿＿＿＿＿＿＿＿＿＿）

☐ ⑦ **PUT TWO AND TWO TOGETHER**　あれこれ総合して推論する
　　＊ 数字を足し算することは考えることに似ている，という発想から。and [to] make [get] four（そして正しい結論を出す）や and [to] make [get] five（そして間違った結論を出す）が続くこともある。

☐ ⑧ **TAKE FIVE**　短い休憩をとる
　　＊ take a five-minute break（5分の休憩をとる）が省略されたイディオム表現。休憩時間は必ずしも5分でなくてもよい。

[A]　辞書定義に合うイディオム表現を選んでみよう。

☐ 1. be doubly profitable = _____

☐ 2. on one's hands and knees = _____

☐ 3. figure something out from the information available
　　= _____

[B]　下線部のイディオム表現の意味に合うものを選んでみよう。

☐ 1. We've been working for three straight hours. Let's take five.
　　(A) take a bite　　　(B) take a day off　　　(C) take a short rest

☐ 2. My room is getting pretty cluttered. I think I'll deep-six these old books.
　　(A) get rid of　　　(B) make use of　　　(C) take care of

☐ 3. The refugees received visas at the eleventh hour, just before the border was closed.
　　(A) at a time　　　(B) at first hand　　　(C) at the last moment

[C]　語句を並べかえ，英文を完成させてみよう。

☐ 1. 自分の車を手に入れたとき，本当にうれしかった。
I [a car / got / heaven / I / in / of / my own / seventh / was really / when].

I _____ .

☐ 2. シャーロック・ホームズは事実や証拠を結びつけて正しい結論を出すのが素早かった。
Sherlock Homes [and / four / put / quick to / together to make / two / two / was].

Sherlock Homes _____ .

[D]　英文を完成させ，日本語に直してみよう。

☐ 1. Our company is really behind the (　　　　) ball. We have a huge debt to pay but can't borrow any more money.

_____

☐ 2. If I go to Chicago next Friday, I can kill (　　　　) birds with one stone. I can attend the conference and visit my mother on the same day.

_____

27

LESSON 12 「衣服」などを用いたイディオム表現

「濡れた毛布を投げる」って何をすること？

LET'S LEARN　下線部を埋め，和訳を完成させてみよう。

- ① **AN ACE UP ONE'S SLEEVE**　切り札；奥の手
  * 昔，ほとんどの服にポケットがついていなかったため，トランプのゲームでいかさま師がエースの切り札を袖の中にしのばせたことから。

- ② **AT THE DROP OF A HAT**　すぐに
  * 西部開拓時代，決闘を開始する合図として，立会人が帽子を落としたことに由来。

- ③ **FLIP ONE'S WIG**　急に怒る；かんしゃくを起こす
  * 「人前でむやみやたらとはずさない自分のカツラを投げる」→「平静な心を失う」
  [例] Stop whistling. You make me flip my wig.
  　　（口笛を吹くのをやめろよ。いらいらしてくる）

- ④ **KEEP ONE'S SHIRT ON**　落ち着いている
  * 昔，シャツは高価なもので，ケンカになると男たちはシャツを脱いだことから。
  [例] Keep your shirt on! We're not completely defeated.
  　　（落ち着け！ 1.＿＿＿＿＿＿＿＿＿＿＿＿＿＿＿＿＿）

- ⑤ **PASS THE HAT**　少額の寄付を集める；お金を出し合う
  * 昔，余興や芝居でパフォーマンスが終わると，主催者や主演者が見物客からお金をもらうために客に帽子を回したことから。
  [例] We passed the hat around for Matilda's birthday present.
  　　（2.＿＿＿＿＿＿＿＿＿＿＿＿＿＿＿＿みんなでお金を出し合った）

- ⑥ **SPEAK OFF THE CUFF**　準備なしで話す
  * 昔，テーブルスピーチで，スピーチの準備ができていないときワイシャツの袖口にメモしたことに由来。

- ⑦ **THROW A WET BLANKET**　座を白けさせる
  * アメリカ先住民が，キャンプの火を消すために近くの川の水に浸した毛布を使ったことに由来。
  [例] His negative attitude threw a wet blanket on our enthusiasm.
  　　（彼の否定的な態度は私たちの熱意に水を差した）

- ⑧ **TIGHTEN ONE'S BELT**　生活を切り詰める
  * 食事を切り詰めて痩せると，ベルトを締め直すことから。
  [例] Now I have to tighten my belt because my rent went up.
  　　（3.＿＿＿＿＿＿＿＿＿＿＿＿＿＿＿＿＿＿＿＿＿）

[A] 辞書定義に合うイディオム表現を選んでみよう。

1. get mad suddenly = _____

2. prevent others from enjoying what they do = _____

3. collect donations of money from people = _____

[B] 下線部のイディオム表現の意味に合うものを選んでみよう。

1. I stuttered badly when I had to speak <u>off the cuff</u>.
   (A) impromptu　　　(B) for myself　　　(C) on my own

2. Many people get divorces these days <u>at the drop of a hat</u>.
   (A) against their will　(B) for a change of pace　(C) easily

3. <u>Keep your shirt on</u>, Greg! They'll be here in time for the wedding.
   (A) Calm down　　(B) Keep off　　　(C) Take care

[C] 語句を並べかえ，英文を完成させてみよう。

1. 交渉するときには，切り札を隠し持っておくべきだ。
   When [an ace / always / have / negotiating, / should / up / you / your sleeve].

   When _____.

2. 知事はスピーチの用意をしていなかったので，即席でしゃべらなければならなかった。
   The governor [a speech, / had to / hadn't / off the cuff / prepared / speak / so he].

   The governor _____.

[D] 英文を完成させ，日本語に直してみよう。

1. Things are beginning to cost more and more, so it looks like we'll all have to tighten our (　　　　　).

   _____

2. Ted would buy her expensive clothing at the drop of a (　　　　　) and worry about how he pay for it later.

   _____

29

LESSON 13 「道具・武器」を用いたイディオム表現

「丸い穴に四角いくぎ」の人ってどんな人？

LET'S LEARN　下線部を埋め，和訳を完成させてみよう。

☐ ① **A SQUARE PEG IN A ROUND HOLE**　不適任者
　＊「丸い穴に四角いくぎ」→「能力・人物などが地位・職業に合っていないこと」
　＊ a round peg in a square hole（四角い穴に丸いくぎ）とも表現できる。

☐ ② **BITE THE BULLET**　困難に立ち向かう
　＊ 麻酔薬がなかった時代に，戦場で負傷した兵士を手術する際に，痛みから気をそらすために兵士に弾丸をかませたことに由来。
　［例］Be a man. Bite the bullet.
　　　（元気を出しなさい。苦しみに男らしく耐えなさい）

☐ ③ **BURY THE HATCHET**　和解する
　＊ 和睦のしるしに，武器である手斧を土の中に埋めたアメリカ先住民の風習から。
　＊「闘いを始める」は take up the hatchet という。
　［例］We had a big argument last week, but we've decided to bury the hatchet.
　　　（1.＿＿＿＿＿＿＿＿＿＿＿＿＿＿＿＿＿＿　仲直りすることにした）

☐ ④ **DROP A BOMBSHELL**　爆弾発言をする
　＊「爆弾を落とす」→「衝撃的な知らせを言う」
　［例］Andy's wife dropped a bombshell by announcing she was going to divorce him.
　　　（アンディーの妻は 2.＿＿＿＿＿＿＿＿＿＿＿＿＿＿＿＿＿＿　と爆弾発言をした）

☐ ⑤ **HIT THE NAIL ON THE HEAD**　ずばり的を射る
　＊「正確にくぎの頭を打つ」→「ずばり的を射る」
　［例］He doesn't usually get the answers right, but every now and then he hits the nail on the head.
　　　（彼はあまり正解を出すことが少ないが，時々的を得たことを言ってくれる）

☐ ⑥ **HIT THE SACK**　床に就く；寝る
　＊「ベッドのマットレスに就く」→「床に就く」
　＊ マットレスの詰め物として「干し草」が使われていたので，hit the hay ともいう。
　［例］What time do you usually hit the sack?
　　　（3.＿＿＿＿＿＿＿＿＿＿＿＿＿＿＿＿＿＿？）

☐ ⑦ **STICK TO ONE'S GUNS**　一歩も譲らない；自分の立場を固守する
　＊「自分の大砲を離れない」→「頑張って応戦する」

☐ ⑧ **THROW A MONKEY WRENCH INTO THE WORKS**　邪魔する
　＊「機械の作動部分にスパナを投げつける」→「うまくいっている作業を妨害する」

[A]　辞書定義に合うイディオム表現を選んでみよう。

☐ 1. stand up for one's rights = _____

☐ 2. say something that is exactly right or correct = _____

☐ 3. do something that will cause problems or spoil someone's plans

　　= _____

[B]　下線部のイディオム表現の意味に合うものを選んでみよう。

☐ 1. You'll have to bite the bullet and tell the boss about your mistake.
　　(A) be brave　　　(B) be coward　　　(C) be positive

☐ 2. When he hits the sack, he reads for a few minutes, then turns out the light.
　　(A) comes home　　(B) gets to work　　(C) goes to bed

☐ 3. Although he got a job in an auto repair shop, he's a square peg in a round hole.
　　(A) a beginner　　(B) a misfit　　(C) an expert

[C]　語句を並べかえ，英文を完成させてみよう。

☐ 1. 航空会社のストライキで，私たちの休暇の計画が台無しになった。
　　The airline strike [a / into / monkey / our / plans / threw / vacation / wrench].

　　The airline strike _____.

☐ 2. わが社の CEO の突然の辞任は大きな衝撃をもたらした。
　　The CEO [a bombshell / by / company / dropped / of / our / resigning / suddenly].

　　The CEO _____.

[D]　英文を完成させ，日本語に直してみよう。

☐ 1. Mick is sticking to his (_____) and doing that job without help from anyone.

_____

☐ 2. David and his wife argued for days over the family budget, but they finally decided to bury the (_____) and settled on a compromise.

_____

31

LESSON 14 「家具」などを用いたイディオム表現

「戸棚の中の骸骨」って何？

LET'S LEARN　下線部を埋め，和訳を完成させてみよう。

☐ ① **A SKELETON IN THE CLOSET**　家族の秘密；人に知られたくないこと
  * 戸棚の中にある骸骨に，毎晩キスをするように夫に命じられた夫人の話に由来。
  [例] My father was in jail for a day once. That's the skeleton in our closet.
  　　（1.＿＿＿＿＿＿＿＿＿＿＿＿＿＿＿＿＿＿。そのことは家族の秘密だ）

☐ ② **EVERYTHING BUT THE KITCHEN SINK**　何でもかんでも
  * 固定されているキッチンの流し以外の物なら，何でも運び出せるという発想から。
  [例] She went away for a holiday, taking everything but the kitchen sink.
  　　（彼女はたくさんの物を持って休暇を過ごしに出かけた）

☐ ③ **GET UP ON THE WRONG SIDE OF THE BED**　朝，気分悪く起きる
  * ベッドの左側から起きると縁起が悪いとされたことから。
  * get out of the wrong side of the bed とも表現できる。

☐ ④ **ON THE EDGE OF ONE'S SEAT**　わくわくしながら見守って
  * スポーツ観戦などで，興奮してくると身を乗り出して自分の席の端にいることから。
  [例] The movie had me on the edge of my seat from start to finish.
  　　（その映画は最初から最後まで夢中になって見ていたわ）

☐ ⑤ **PULL THE RUG OUT FROM ～**　～の計画を台無しにする
  * 「誰かが載っている絨毯を引っぱり取ってしまう」→「計画を邪魔する」

☐ ⑥ **SWEEP ～ UNDER THE RUG**　～を隠す
  * ゴミやチリを見られたくないため，じゅうたんの下に掃き入れてしまう行為から。
  * sweep ～ under the carpet とも表現できる。
  [例] In many schools, drug use by students is swept under the rug.
  　　（多くの学校では，生徒による薬物使用をひた隠しにしている）

☐ ⑦ **TURN THE TABLES**　形勢を逆転する
  * この tables はチェスなどの「ボード」を意味し，負けている時にこれを回転させれば，形勢が逆転することから。
  [例] I was winning the match at first, but the tables turned and I lost.
  　　（2.＿＿＿＿＿＿＿＿＿＿＿＿＿＿＿＿＿＿，形勢が逆転し負けてしまった）

☐ ⑧ **UNDER THE TABLE**　こっそりと；違法に
  * テーブルの下は，こっそりと賄賂を渡す場所としてふさわしいことから。
  [例] The president transferred his property to his sons under the table.
  　　（3.＿＿＿＿＿＿＿＿＿＿＿＿＿＿＿＿＿を違法に譲渡した）

[A]　辞書定義に合うイディオム表現を選んでみよう。

1. change the situation = _____

2. watching ~ with excitement = _____

3. a hidden and shocking secret = _____

[B]　下線部のイディオム表現の意味に合うものを選んでみよう。

1. I heard our manger decided to <u>pull the rug out from under us</u>.
   (A) accept our plan　　(B) admit our plan　　(C) ruin our plan

2. The scandal was <u>swept under the rug</u> because of the politicians involved in it.
   (A) covered up　　(B) created　　(C) uncovered

3. He is unusually grouchy. He must have <u>gotten up on the wrong side of the bed</u> today.
   (A) been in a bed temper　(B) been terribly sleepy　(C) been very tired

[C]　語句を並べかえ，英文を完成させてみよう。

1. おばあちゃんはよくこっそりとお小遣いをくれる。
   My grandma [extra / gives / me / spending money / often / the table / under].

   My grandma _____ .

2. 彼の怖いおばけ話を子どもたちは身を乗り出して聞き入っていた。
   His [ghost stories / kept / of / on / scary / the children / the edge / their seats].

   His _____ .

[D]　英文を完成させ，日本語に直してみよう。

1. What's the matter? Did you get up on the wrong side of the (　　　　　) or something?

   _____

2. Bill orders everything but the kitchen (　　　　　) when he goes out to dinner, especially when someone else is paying for it.

   _____

33

LESSON 15 「家屋」などを用いたイディオム表現

「頭が天井にぶつかる」ってどうなること？

LET'S LEARN 下線部を埋め，和訳を完成させてみよう。

☐ ① **A PILLAR OF STRENGTH** 精神的支柱；惜しみなく支援をしてくれる大黒柱

＊「重い屋根を支える柱」→「支援し励ましてくれるもの」

［例］Our company has been a pillar of strength in this community for years.
（わが社は何年もの間，この地域で惜しみなく支援を続けてきた）

☐ ② **BRING THE HOUSE DOWN** 聴衆から大喝采を受ける

＊ この house は「劇場」を意味し，劇場が倒壊するくらいの拍手喝采を受けるというイメージから。

［例］That comedian brings the house down whenever he tells a joke.
（1. _____ いつでも大うけだ）

☐ ③ **DRIVE ～ UP THE WALL** イライラさせる；逆上させる

＊「人を壁の上に追いやる」→「追い詰めてイライラさせる」

［例］The noise is enough to drive anyone up the wall.
（その騒音は誰をもイライラさせるほどひどいものだった）

☐ ④ **GO DOWN THE DRAIN** 無駄になる；水の泡となる

＊「排水路に流れて行く」→「永遠になくなってしまう」

［例］In the end, all our efforts went down the drain.
（結局，私たちの努力はすべて水の泡となってしまった）

☐ ⑤ **HIT HOME** 実感させる；核心をつく

＊「家」は誰にとっても大切なところであることから「痛いところをつく」の意味に。

［例］His message seemed to hit home with most people who watched him on TV.
（彼のメッセージはテレビを見ていたほとんどの人の心を打ったようだ）

☐ ⑥ **HIT THE CEILING** カンカンに怒る

＊ カッと怒って飛び上がった拍子に，頭が天井にぶつかるイメージから。

［例］My dad will hit the ceiling when he finds out that I wrecked his car.
（私が 2. _____ ，父はカンカンに怒るだろう）

☐ ⑦ **ON THE HOUSE** 店のおごりで

＊ この house は「飲食店」，on は「～もちで」という意味。

［例］You only need to pay for your meal. Drinks are on the house tonight.
（3. _____ 。今夜，飲み物はただなんだ）

☐ ⑧ **SHOW THE DOOR** 辞めてもらう

＊「ドアはこちらです，どうぞここから出て行ってください」というしぐさから。

[A]　辞書定義に合うイディオム表現を選んでみよう。

1. get really mad = _____

2. make someone quit one's company = _____

3. make someone really feel something = _____

[B]　下線部のイディオム表現の意味に合うものを選んでみよう。

1. "Here," said the waitress, "have a glass of wine on the house."
   (A) for free　　　　(B) in addition　　　　(C) in no time

2. All my work went down the drain when a fire destroyed my office.
   (A) was completed　　(B) was left behind　　(C) was destroyed

3. Working in front of a computer screen all day drives me up the wall.
   (A) irritates me　　(B) leaves me alone　　(C) makes me motivated

[C]　語句を並べかえ，英文を完成させてみよう。

1. 大統領は，国の精神的支柱でなければならない。
   The president [a pillar / for / of / serve as / should / strength / the nation].

   The president _____.

2. 足首を捻挫してしまい，私のオリンピックへの夢は泡と消えた。
   When I [all my / down / my ankle, / Olympic hopes / sprained / the drain / went].

   When I _____.

[D]　英文を完成させ，日本語に直してみよう。

1. I went to a restaurant last night. I was the 10,000th customer, and my dinner was on the (　　　　　).

   _____

2. When our principal came out on stage dressed like a high school student, she brought the (　　　　　) down.

   _____

LESSON 16　「食べ物」を用いたイディオム表現

「ひとくちのケーキ」って何？

LET'S LEARN　下線部を埋め，和訳を完成させてみよう。

☐ ① **A BIG CHEESE**　重要人物

* この cheese は食べるチーズではなくて，ヒンディー語で「もの」を意味する chiz に由来する。植民地時代，イギリス人がインドで英語に取り入れたことから。

［例］Apparently his father is a big cheese in one of the major banks.
（明らかに，彼のお父さんは大銀行の重要人物だ）

☐ ② **A PIECE OF CAKE**　朝飯前のこと

* as easy as eating a piece of cake（ひとくちのケーキを食べるくらい簡単な）に由来。

［例］Can you finish this by noon?—Sure. It's a piece of cake.
（「これ，正午までにできますか？」「もちろんです。お安い御用です」）

☐ ③ **BE FULL OF BEANS**　活気に満ちている

*「馬がエサの豆を腹いっぱい食べている」→「元気いっぱいである」

☐ ④ **BE PACKED LIKE SARDINES**　混雑して

* イワシの缶詰にイワシがぎっしり詰まっていることから。

［例］Every year many trains are packed like sardines during summer vacation.
（1.＿＿＿＿＿＿＿＿＿＿＿＿＿＿＿＿＿＿＿はすし詰め状態だ）

☐ ⑤ **BE SMALL POTATOES**　たいしたことではない

*「少量のジャガイモ」→「重要でない」

☐ ⑥ **GO BANANAS**　すぐ怒る；ひどく興奮する

* サルが大好物のバナナを目の前にすると，すごく興奮することから。

［例］Mom will go bananas if she sees this mess.
（2.＿＿＿＿＿＿＿＿＿＿＿＿＿＿＿＿＿＿＿ママはかっとくるだろうな）

☐ ⑦ **ONE'S BREAD AND BUTTER**　主要な収入源

*「パンとバター」→「飯の種」

［例］Selling cars is a lot of hard work, but it's my bread and butter.
（3.＿＿＿＿＿＿＿＿＿＿＿＿＿＿＿＿＿＿＿，それが私の生業なのだ）

☐ ⑧ **PUT ALL ONE'S EGGS IN ONE BASKET**　1つにすべてを賭ける

* 卵がいっぱい入ったカゴを落としたら，卵は全部割れてしまうことから。

［例］We should spread our investments over several companies. It wouldn't be wise to put all our eggs in one basket.
（投資先を数社に分けるべきだ。1社だけにすべてをかけるのは賢明なやり方ではない）

36

LET'S TRY

[A] 辞書定義に合うイディオム表現を選んでみよう。

☐ 1. be pressed tightly together = _____

☐ 2. risk losing everything at one time = _____

☐ 3. an important or powerful person in a group or organization
= _____

[B] 下線部のイディオム表現の意味に合うものを選んでみよう。

☐ 1. I've never met anyone so full of beans before breakfast.
(A) energetic　　　(B) exhausted　　　(C) overweight

☐ 2. When her favorite team won the championship, she went bananas.
(A) felt sad　　　(B) kept cool　　　(C) was overcome with joy

☐ 3. Our team is strong, so it will be a piece of cake to make it to the finals.
(A) almost impossible　　(B) quite difficult　　(C) very easy

[C] 語句を並べかえ，英文を完成させてみよう。

☐ 1. 会社が倒産したら，主要な収入源を失ってしまう。
If [and / bankrupt, / bread / butter / goes / I'll / lose / my / the company].

If _____ .

☐ 2. 彼は日本語を上手に話すけど，スーに比べたらたいしたことない。
He [but / good Japanese, / it's / compared / Sue / small potatoes / speaks / with].

He _____ .

[D] 英文を完成させ，日本語に直してみよう。

☐ 1. I've never known a boy to be so full of (　　　　　). He runs around laughing and playing all day long.

_____

☐ 2. I hate getting the train in the morning. We're all packed in like (　　　　　) and it's always hot and smelly.

_____

37

LESSON 17 「飲食」を用いたイディオム表現 (1)

「酸っぱいブドウ」って何？

LET'S LEARN　下線部を埋め，和訳を完成させてみよう。

☐ ① **BE NOT ONE'S CUP OF TEA**　〜の好みではない；〜が得意ではない

　　＊「大好きな1杯のお茶」→「自分の気に入ったもの」
　　＊ 紅茶好きが多いイギリスの古いイディオム表現。
　　［例］That kind of movie is not my cup of tea.
　　　　（1.＿＿＿＿＿＿＿＿＿＿＿＿＿＿＿＿＿＿＿＿）

☐ ② **BRING HOME THE BACON**　生活の糧を稼ぐ；成功を収める

　　＊ 昔，スポーツの試合で入賞すると，賞品としてベーコンが与えられたことに由来。
　　［例］I want to marry a steady, reliable man who will always bring home the bacon.
　　　　（いつもきちんと生活の糧を稼いでくれる堅実で信頼できる男性と結婚したい）

☐ ③ **CUT THE MUSTARD**　期待に添う

　　＊ この the mustard は「鋭い味の物」から「本質的なもの」を意味する。
　　［例］Even though she studied hard, she just couldn't cut the mustard.
　　　　（2.＿＿＿＿＿＿＿＿＿＿＿＿＿＿＿＿＿＿，彼女は期待通りに成果を上げられなかった）

☐ ④ **IN A NUTSHELL**　要するに

　　＊ nutshell（ナッツの殻）は小さい物の代表で，「それに入る」というイメージから。
　　［例］What he said was, in a nutshell, nonsense.
　　　　（彼の話は，要するに，ナンセンスだった）

☐ ⑤ **SELL LIKE HOTCAKES**　飛ぶように売れる

　　＊ この hotcakes は「人気のケーキ」で，日本語の「ホットケーキ」は a pancake。
　　［例］This new video game is selling like hotcakes.
　　　　（この新しいビデオゲームは飛ぶように売れています）

☐ ⑥ **SOUR GRAPES**　負け惜しみ

　　＊ キツネがおいしそうなブドウを取ろうとしたが，手が届かないので「どうせ酸っぱいブドウだ」と言ったイソップ物語（Aesop's Fables）に由来。
　　［例］His comments about the new car are just sour grapes because he can't afford it.
　　　　（3.＿＿＿＿＿＿＿＿＿＿＿＿＿＿＿＿＿　彼には手が届かないための負け惜しみだ）

☐ ⑦ **THE CARROT AND THE STICK**　アメとムチ

　　＊ 好物のニンジンと嫌いなムチをうまく使って，馬を走らせることから。

☐ ⑧ **THE TOP BANANA**　責任者；組織のトップ

　　＊ 3人で演じる喜劇で，しゃれたことを言った役者にバナナが与えられたことに由来。

LET'S TRY

[A]　辞書定義に合うイディオム表現を選んでみよう。

☐ 1. being a bad loser = _____

☐ 2. be not something one prefers = _____

☐ 3. the effective use of two different methods = _____

[B]　下線部のイディオム表現の意味に合うものを選んでみよう。

☐ 1. Those new action figures are selling <u>like hotcakes</u>.
　　(A)　forever　　　　　(B)　helplessly　　　　(C)　very well

☐ 2. Women nowadays not only take care of the household, but <u>bring home the bacon</u> too.
　　(A)　earn a salary　　(B)　play around　　　(C)　stay home

☐ 3. I'd like to say a lot more, but to put it <u>in a nutshell</u>, his plan was a complete failure.
　　(A)　in advance　　　(B)　in general　　　　(C)　in short

[C]　語句を並べかえ，英文を完成させてみよう。

☐ 1. 彼はアメとムチ方式を上手く使い，政策を推し進めていった。
　　He [and / his policy / pursuing / the carrot / stick / approach in / used].

　　He _____.

☐ 2. エドとぼくは，エドが社長になるまでは親しい友人同士だった。
　　Ed [and I / he became / close friends / the company's / top banana / until / were].

　　Ed _____.

[D]　英文を完成させ，日本語に直してみよう。

☐ 1. You two visit the art museum without me. Looking at fussy old paintings is not my cup of (　　　　　).

_____

☐ 2. He was 42 and many people thought he was too old to cut the (　　　　　), but he hit forty homeruns.

_____

39

LESSON 18 「飲食」を用いたイディオム表現 (2)

「リンゴを磨く」って何をすること？

LET'S LEARN　下線部を埋め，和訳を完成させてみよう。

☐ ① **A TOUGH NUT TO CRACK**　厄介な問題；難問題

　＊「割れ目を入れるのが難しい」→「取っかかりをつかむのが難しい」

　＊ a hard nut to crack とも表現できる。

　〔例〕The trouble they have is a tough nut to crack.
　　　　（1._____は解く糸口をつかむのが難しい）

☐ ② **BE NUTTY AS A FRUITCAKE**　おかしい；どうかしている

　＊ nuts には「気が狂った」という意味があり，フルーツケーキにはナッツがたくさん入っていることから。

☐ ③ **BE PIE IN THE SKY**　絵に描いた餅である

　＊「手に取って食べられない空に浮かぶパイ」→「はかない夢」

　〔例〕You expect to get rich from this scheme, but it's just pie in the sky.
　　　　（この計画で金持ちになろうとしているけど，それはただの絵に描いた餅だよ）

☐ ④ **BE WORTH *ONE'S* SALT**　給料に恥じない働きがある；有能である

　＊ ローマ時代に，兵士に給料の一部として「塩」が支給されたことに由来。

　〔例〕I think he's more than worth his salt. He's a good worker.
　　　　（彼は給料以上の働きがあると思う。2._____）

☐ ⑤ **BEEF UP ～**　～を強化する

　＊ 牛肉を食べると力が出ることから。

　〔例〕The professor beefed up his lecture with more examples.
　　　　（教授はもっと実例を挙げることによって，講義をより充実したものにした）

☐ ⑥ **COME HOME WITH THE MILK**　朝帰りをする

　＊ 帰宅時間が朝の牛乳配達の時間と同じになることから。

☐ ⑦ **FROM SOUP TO NUTS**　何から何まで

　＊ スープに始まり，ナッツを使った物が多いデザートで終わるフルコース料理に由来。

　〔例〕Today's drugstores have everything from soup to nuts.
　　　　（最近のドラッグストアには何から何までそろっている）

☐ ⑧ **POLISH THE APPLE**　ゴマをする

　＊ アメリカの小学生が，先生のご機嫌をとり成績を上げてもらおうと，ピカピカに磨いたリンゴを差し出した習慣から。「ゴマをする人」は an apple-polisher という。

　〔例〕I hate to see someone polishing the apple.
　　　　（3._____のが嫌いだ）

LET'S TRY

[A] 辞書定義に合うイディオム表現を選んでみよう。

◯ 1. strengthen or build up = _____

◯ 2. a difficult problem to solve = _____

◯ 3. stay out all night and return home on the following morning
   = _____

[B] 下線部のイディオム表現の意味に合うものを選んでみよう。

◯ 1. This encyclopedia includes everything <u>from soup to nuts</u>.
   (A) from A to Z　　　(B) from one to ten　　　(C) the ABC

◯ 2. She's <u>nutty as a fruitcake</u>. She wore her swimsuit to class!
   (A) crazy　　　(B) cute　　　(C) informal

◯ 3. Thomas <u>polished the apple around</u> the boss and was promoted to section chief.
   (A) argued with　　　(B) flattered　　　(C) made up with

[C] 語句を並べかえ，英文を完成させてみよう。

◯ 1. 夫がまた朝帰りをしたので，こってり絞ってやったわ。
   My husband [came / chewed him / home / I / out / so / the milk again, / with].

   My husband _____.

◯ 2. 一度彼と話をすれば，頭がおかしいことがわかるだろう。
   Once [a fruitcake / as / he / him, / is / nutty / realize that / talk to / you / you'll].

   Once _____.

[D] 英文を完成させ，日本語に直してみよう。

◯ 1. The promises of political reform turned out to be nothing but
   (_____) in the sky.

   _____

◯ 2. Sam showed that he was worth his (_____) as a car salesperson by selling ten cars during his first month on the job.

   _____

41

LESSON 19 「身体」を用いたイディオム表現 (1)

「全部の指が親指」の人ってどんな人？

LET'S LEARN　下線部を埋め，和訳を完成させてみよう。

☐ ① **A PAIN IN THE NECK**　悩みの種
　＊首が痛い時は，思うように行動や仕事ができないことから。
　［例］Vincent is a pain in the neck. He is not cooperative.
　　　（ビンセントが悩みの種なんだ。彼って協力的でないからね）

☐ ② **A SHOT IN THE ARM**　元気のもと
　＊「腕に打った皮下注射」→「絶好の刺激剤」
　［例］Thank you for cheering me up. It was a real shot in the arm.
　　　（1.　　　　　　　　　　　　　　　　。本当に励ましになりました）

☐ ③ **BE ALL THUMBS**　手先が不器用である
　＊「全部の指が親指である」→「手を使ってする仕事がうまくできない」

☐ ④ **GET COLD FEET**　怖気づく；恐れをなす
　＊恐怖は血行を悪くし，足が凍りついたようになって先に進めないイメージから。
　［例］I want to ask her out, but I always get cold feet, and can't even speak to her.
　　　（2.　　　　　　　　　　　　　　　　，いつも怖気づいてしまい話しかけられない）

☐ ⑤ **GET THE THUMBS UP**　許可を得る
　＊ローマ時代の奴隷の格闘技で，勝敗が決まると敗者の奴隷をどうするかを観客に尋ねた。観客が親指を立てると敗者は勇敢に戦ったとされ寛大な処置を受け，親指を立てないと敗者は直ちに処刑されたことに由来。
　［例］Her proposal got the thumbs up from the party.
　　　（彼女の提案は党の賛成を得た）

☐ ⑥ **GIVE ～ A SHOULDER TO CRY ON**　～をなぐさめる
　＊人をなぐさめる時，その上で泣くための肩を差し出すという行為から。

☐ ⑦ **KEEP ONE'S FINGERS CROSSED**　よい結果を祈る
　＊「十字架が厄払いになる」という迷信に由来。指を交差させた手の甲を，これから大事な試験を受けたりする人に向けて，I'll keep my fingers crossed for you. という。
　［例］I'm going for a job interview today. Keep your fingers crossed for me.
　　　（3.　　　　　　　　　　　　　　　　。成功を祈っていてね）

☐ ⑧ **SHOW ONE'S HAND**　手の内を明かす：真意を明かす
　＊この hand は「トランプの持ち札」。
　［例］You shouldn't show your hand until the end in business negotiations.
　　　（商売の交渉では，最後まで手の内を見せないほうがいいよ）

LET'S TRY

[A] 辞書定義に合うイディオム表現を選んでみよう。

1. a big headache = _____

2. gain permission = _____

3. reveal one's intentions to someone = _____

[B] 下線部のイディオム表現の意味に合うものを選んでみよう。

1. Thank you for <u>giving me a shoulder to cry on</u> last night.
   (A) cheering me up　　(B) making it up to me　　(C) picking me up

2. I'm afraid I'm <u>all thumbs</u> when it comes to fixing things.
   (A) clever　　　　　　(B) skillful　　　　　　　(C) clumsy

3. I had agreed to go rock climbing, but I began to <u>get cold feet</u> at the last minute.
   (A) become timid　　　(B) feel at ease　　　　　(C) get excited

[C] 語句を並べかえ，英文を完成させてみよう。

1. 私の1週間の休暇願が上司に認められた。
   My request [a week's / for / got / leave / the boss / the thumbs / up from].

   My request _____.

2. 彼女に話しかけたいが，いつも土壇場で怖気づいてしまう。
   I [at / but / cold feet / get / her, / I always / talk to / the last moment / want to].

   I _____.

[D] 英文を完成させ，日本語に直してみよう。

1. I was feeling pretty low in the hospital, but your card really gave me a shot in the (　　　　　).

   _____

2. I don't know whether Vincent is intending to marry Sally or not. He's not one to show his (　　　　　).

   _____

43

LESSON 20　「身体」を用いたイディオム表現 (2)

「耳の後ろが濡れている」ってどういうこと？

LET'S LEARN　下線部を埋め，和訳を完成させてみよう。

☐ ① **BE ALL EARS**　熱心に聞く
* 「全身を耳にしている」→「聞きたくてウズウズしている」

［例］Do you want to hear what happened at the party?—Oh, yes. I'm all ears.
　　（「1.＿＿＿＿＿＿＿＿＿＿＿＿＿＿＿＿＿＿＿？」「ええ，ぜひとも聞かせて」）

☐ ② **BE ON *ONE'S* TOES**　気を抜かずにやる；油断なく身構えている
* テニスなどのスポーツで敏速に動けるようにつま先立ちして，事態の変化にいつでも対処できるように構える姿勢から。

☐ ③ **BE WET BEHIND THE EARS**　未熟である
* 動物が生まれたての時は羊水で体中が濡れていて，体はすぐに乾き始めるが，耳の後ろの小さなくぼみは最後まで濡れていることから。
* 逆の意味の表現に be dry behind the ears がある。

［例］The job put a lot of responsibility on someone who was still wet behind the ears.
　　（その仕事はまだ未熟な人には 2.＿＿＿＿＿＿＿＿＿＿＿＿＿＿＿＿＿＿＿）

☐ ④ **BY WORD OF MOUTH**　くちコミで
* 「口の言葉で」→「活字でなくくちづてで」

☐ ⑤ **KEEP AN EAR TO THE GROUND**　気を配る；情勢を敏感にとらえている
* アメリカ先住民と白人の間で争いごとが絶えない時代，主な移動手段が馬車だったため，敵が来ると地面に耳をつけて相手との距離や人数を知ろうとしたことから。

☐ ⑥ **KEEP *ONE'S* NOSE TO THE GRINDSTONE**　こつこつ働く
* 粉を挽いたり砥石で研いだりするときに，鼻を臼や砥石にくっつけるようにして働く様子から。

☐ ⑦ **ON THE TIP OF *ONE'S* TONGUE**　言いたいことがのど元まで出かかって
* 「言いたいことが舌先にある」→「言いたいことがのど元まできている」
* 英語では「舌」がしゃべることを象徴する。

［例］Her name was on the tip of my tongue, but I couldn't quite get it.
　　（彼女の名前が出かかっていたんだが，3.＿＿＿＿＿＿＿＿＿＿＿＿＿＿＿＿＿＿＿）

☐ ⑧ **TURN A BLIND EYE TO ～**　～に目をつぶる；～を見て見ぬふりをする
* コペンハーゲンの海戦でネルソン提督がデンマーク艦隊の接近を前に，見えない方の目に望遠鏡をあててこれを無視し，その後の海戦でデンマーク軍を降伏に追い込んだことに由来する。
* 類似表現に，turn a deaf ear to ～（～に耳を貸さない）がある。

LET'S TRY

[A] 辞書定義に合うイディオム表現を選んでみよう。

1. be young and inexperienced = _____

2. listen carefully, hoping to get advance warning of something
   = _____

3. be eager to listen to something, especially if it will benefit you
   = _____

[B] 下線部のイディオム表現の意味に合うものを選んでみよう。

1. You have to <u>be on your toes</u> if you want to succeed.
   (A) keep alert　　　　(B) run a risk　　　　(C) take a chance

2. I <u>have his name on the tip of my tongue</u>, but I can't recall it.
   (A) almost remember his name　(B) forget his name　　(C) know his name

3. He told me to <u>keep my nose to the grindstone</u> or he'll find someone else to do my job.
   (A) give him a hand　　(B) take a break　　(C) work hard

[C] 語句を並べかえ，英文を完成させてみよう。

1. 飢えている子どもたちを目にして見ぬふりはできないでしょ？
   How [a blind / all those / can / children / eye / starving / to / turn / you]?
   How _____?

2. その映画の前評判はよくなかったが，くちコミで人気が出てきた。
   The movie [bad reviews, / became / but it / through word / got / mouth / of / popular].
   The movie _____.

[D] 英文を完成させ，日本語に直してみよう。

1. When he started telling about his experience in Africa, the kids were all (　　　　　　).
   _____

2. The city government turned a blind (　　　　　　) to the illegal dumping that was going on in the park next to the high school.
   _____

45

MEMO

著作権法上、無断複写・複製は禁じられています。

A Shorter Course in English Idiomatic Expressions　　[B-793]
5分間　英語イディオム表現
1　刷　2015年1月15日

著　者	小中　秀彦　　　　　　Hidehiko Konaka
発行者	南雲　一範　　Kazunori Nagumo
発行所	株式会社　南雲堂
	〒162-0801　東京都新宿区山吹町361
	NAN'UN-DO Co., Ltd.
	361 Yamabuki-cho, Shinjuku-ku, Tokyo 162-0801, Japan
	振替口座：00160-0-46863
	TEL: 03-3268-2311(代表)／FAX: 03-3269-2486
編　集	加藤　敦
製　版	木内　早苗
装　丁	Nスタジオ
検　印	省　略
コード	ISBN 978-4-523-17793-7　C0082

Printed in Japan

E-mail　nanundo@post.email.ne.jp
URL　http://www.nanun-do.co.jp/

南雲堂

好評！英語リーディング教材

英語リーディングの王道
The Royal Road to Current English Reading

著　Jim Knudsen
解説　小中秀彦

A5判 173ページ
別冊（A5判 139ページ）

定価（本体1,900円＋税）

アフリカの貧困や病気、核兵器や地雷、ゲームが人に与える影響……。社会における最新事情、政治や歴史などの大きなテーマから日常的な話題に至るまで、現代社会を理解するために必要とされるグローバルな視点を養う英文で各種試験に応用できる真のリーディング力を身につけよう！！

練習問題が充実！
基本的な内容理解に役立ち、生きた英語が身に付く。

CD(MP3)付！
繰り返し聴いて何度も練習できる。

別冊解答付！
全文日本語訳対応。丁寧でわかりやすい解説。

内容

Lesson 1	What the World Needs Now
Lesson 2	The Horns of a Dilemma
Lesson 3	Of Nukes and Minefields
Lesson 4	Languages Lost and Found
Lesson 5	It's About Time
Lesson 6	Where Would We Be Without It?
Lesson 7	Virtually Better
Lesson 8	It's Never Too Late
Lesson 9	Global Concepts 1: People
Lesson 10	Global Concepts 2: Trends
Lesson 11	Psychology
Lesson 12	The Environment
Lesson 13	History
Lesson 14	Space
Lesson 15	Education
Vocabulary	
Verbal Constructions and Phrases	

南雲堂
〒162-0801
東京都新宿区山吹町361
TEL: 03-3268-2384
FAX: 03-3260-5425